MICHAEL MORPURGO was born in St Albans in 1943. After a short time with the army, he took up teaching and started to write. He has written many books for children, five of which have been made into films. He also writes screenplays and libretti for opera. He and his wife have set up the children's charity, 'Farms for City Children'. In 1999 this work was publicly recognised when he and his wife were awarded an MBE for services to youth.

Morpurgo's books include *Out of the Ashes* (2001); *Why the Whales Came* (1985), which was made into a film starring Helen Mirren; *King of the Cloud Forests* (1988), which won the Cercle D'Or Prix Sorcière (France); *My Friend Walter* (1988) and *Out of the Ashes* (2001), which were both adapted for television. *The Wreck of the Zanzibar* (1995) won the 1995 Whitbread Children's Book Award.

The Butterfly Lion (1996) won the 1996 Nestlé Smarties Book Prize (Gold Award). *Kensuke's Kingdom* (1999) won the Children's Book Award in 2000. *Private Peaceful* (2003) won the 2005 Red House Children's Book Award and the Blue Peter Book of the Year Award and was shortlisted for the 2004 Whitbread Children's Book Award.

In 2003 Michael Morpurgo became the third Children's Laureate. He was awarded an OBE in 2006 for services to literature.

D0094098

STUART PATERSON

Stuart Paterson's children's plays, first performed at Glasgow
Citizens' Theatre, Edinburgh Royal Lyceum, Dundee Repertory
Theatre, Newcastle Playhouse and Birmingham Old Rep, have
since been staged throughout the UK, and also in Holland,
Norway, Sweden and Finland. They include
*Merlin the Magnificent, Beauty and the Beast, Cinderella,
Granny and the Gorilla, The Sleeping Beauty, Hansel and Gretel,
Puss in Boots*, the one-act play *The Secret Voice*, and adaptations
of Hans Christian Andersen's *The Snow Queen*, George
MacDonald's *The Princess and the Goblin*, Roald Dahl's
George's Marvellous Medicine, J.M. Barrie's *Peter Pan*, Rudyard
Kipling's *The Jungle Book*, and Michael Morpurgo's *Kensuke's
Kingdom. Hansel and Gretel* and *Kensuke's Kingdom* were both
nominated for the Barclay's Best Children's Play of the Year
Award.

He has written *King of the Fields* for the Traverse Theatre, and
new versions of Chekhov's *The Cherry Orchard, Uncle Vanya*
and *The Seagull*. For the Scottish Youth Theatre he has written *In
Traction* (later televised by the BBC) and adapted Zola's
Germinal. He has also adapted Zola's *Thérèse Raquin* for
Communicado Theatre Company, which was later staged at
Newcastle Playhouse where his adaptation of William Trevor's
The Ballroom of Romance was also produced. He has recently
completed a new version of *Comrades* by August Strindberg, a
new play, *Moon Street*, and a children's book, *Silversand*.

Television credits include *The Old Course* and the film
Workhorses, which won the BBC Pharic McLaren Award for best
script and best production. The short film *Somebody's Wee
Nobody* won the Gold Award at the Chicago International Film
Festival. Other film projects include original screenplays *The
Pretender, Whisky Mac, Under the Same Moon* and screen
adaptations of *The Kelpie's Pearls* by Mollie Hunter, *Fergus
Lamont* by Robin Jenkins, and *Scandal* by Shusaku Endo.

Stuart has also written *Misterstourworm* and a short-story version
of his play of *Hansel and Gretel* as narratives for classical
compositions by Savourna Stevenson.

Michael Morpurgo

KENSUKE'S KINGDOM

adapted for the stage by

STUART PATERSON

NICK HERN BOOKS
London
www.nickhernbooks.co.uk

A Nick Hern Book

This adaptation of *Kensuke's Kingdom* first published in Great Britain in 2006 as a paperback original by Nick Hern Books Limited, The Glasshouse, 49a Goldhawk Road, London W12 8QP

Reprinted 2008, 2009, 2011, 2012

This adaptation of *Kensuke's Kingdom* copyright © 2006 Stuart Paterson and Michael Morpurgo

Original book by Michael Morpurgo copyright © 1999 Michael Morpurgo

Stuart Paterson has asserted his right to be identified as the author of this work

Cover image: feastcreative.com
Cover design: Ned Hoste, 2H

Typeset by Country Setting, Kingsdown, Kent CT14 8ES
Printed and bound in Great Britain by CPI Antony Rowe, Chippenham, Wiltshire

A CIP catalogue record for this book is available from the British Library

ISBN 978 1 85459 969 8

CAUTION   All rights whatsoever in this play are strictly reserved. Requests to reproduce the text in whole or in part should be addressed to the publisher.

Amateur Performing Rights   Applications for performance by amateurs, including readings and excerpts, in the English language throughout the world (and by stock companies in the United States of America and Canada) should be addressed to the Performing Rights Manager, Nick Hern Books, The Glasshouse, 49a Goldhawk Road, London W12 8QP, *tel* +44 (0)20 8749 4953, *e-mail* info@nickhernbooks.co.uk, except as follows:

Australia: Dominie Drama, 8 Cross Street, Brookvale 2100, *fax* (2) 9938 8695, *e-mail* drama@dominie.com.au

New Zealand: Play Bureau, PO Box 420, New Plymouth, *fax* (6) 753 2150, *e-mail* play.bureau.nz@xtra.co.nz

South Africa: DALRO (pty) Ltd, PO Box 31627, 2017 Braamfontein, *tel* (11) 712 8000, *fax* (11) 403 9094, *e-mail* theatricals@dalro.co.za

Professional Performing Rights   Application for performance by professionals in any medium and in any language throughout the world should be addressed to Alan Brodie Representation Ltd, Paddock Suite, The Courtyard, 55a Charterhouse Street, London EC1M 6HA, *fax* +44 (0)20 7183 7999, *web* www.alanbrodie.com

No performance of any kind may be given unless a licence has been obtained. Applications should be made before rehearsals begin. Publication of this play does not necessarily indicate its availability for amateur performance.

MIX
Paper from responsible sources
FSC
www.fsc.org   FSC® C013604

For Ella and Johnny

This adaptation of *Kensuke's Kingdom* was first performed by the Birmingham Stage Company at the Birmingham Old Rep on 16 November 2005, followed by a national tour, with the following cast:

KENSUKE	Ozzie Yu
MICHAEL	Iain Ridley
FATHER / TOMODACHI	Mark Carleton
MOTHER / ORANG-UTAN	Julia Hickman
STELLA ARTOIS	Anna Drayson
GRANDMOTHER / KIKANBO	Hannah Birkin
ORANG-UTAN / HUNTER / MICHIYA	Neil Suarez

Director Greg Banks
Designer Jacqueline Trousdale
Lighting Jason Taylor
Music Matthew Scott
Sound Tom Lishman
Movement Peter Elliot

KENSUKE'S KINGDOM

Michael Morpurgo

adapted by Stuart Paterson

Characters

Michael's FATHER

MICHAEL, *a twelve-year-old boy*

Michael's MOTHER

STELLA ARTOIS, *the family dog*

Michael's GRANDMOTHER

TOMODACHI, *a mother orang-utan*

KENSUKE, *an old man*

KIKANBO, *a young orang-utan, Tomodachi's son*

HUNTER

MICHIYA

ACT ONE

Scene One

1987. Inside a repair shed which houses a huge, mysterious object shrouded in sheets. The sound of seagulls calling from outside. Michael's FATHER *paces nervously, looking at his watch, talking to himself.*

FATHER. All you have to do is tell them the truth. No one can argue with the truth . . . (*Panics.*) They'll be here any minute . . . They'll hate me, think I've gone mad . . . Come on! You're a grown man – time to act like one. (*Stands up straight, takes deep breaths.*) Man . . . Grown man . . . That's more like it . . . (*The sound of a car pulling up outside. His courage evaporates in an instant.*) They're here . . . How am I going to tell them? They're here!

Enter MICHAEL.

Michael . . .

MICHAEL (*unsure, a little distantly*). Dad.

FATHER. It's so good to see you, Monkey-Face, you've no idea how good . . . Where's your mother?

MICHAEL. She's paying the taxi.

FATHER. Of course she is . . .

MICHAEL. Why did you go away, Dad? What is this place? What's going on?

Before he can answer Michael's MOTHER *enters with the family dog,* STELLA ARTOIS.

FATHER (*exuberantly, throwing his arms wide*). Stella! (*The dog bounds happily over to him.*) Oh, you beautiful girl! Stella Artois! Yes, you are beautiful. (*Makes her roll over, scratches her ears and tummy, makes a real fuss of her. His wife watches him coldly.*) And so clever, so very, very clever . . . Good dog, yes you are, clever girl . . .

MOTHER (*with distilled fury*). Oh yes, you can talk to the dog, but you've got nothing to say to your own family! We've been hours on a train, paid a fortune for a taxi to God knows where, and I'm telling you right now, James Farrow, you'd better have something to say to us, or we'll be gone before you can . . . We'll be gone . . .

Tears threaten, and she turns away.

FATHER. Don't cry, Linda . . .

MOTHER. Don't you 'don't cry' me!

FATHER. Listen, just listen . . . It's like I said on the phone. Everything's going to be all right . . . Wait till you see. I've got it all sorted, the whole thing . . . Mapped out in my head . . . And there's no use you trying to talk me out of it . . .

MOTHER. What?

FATHER. That's what I'm trying to tell you.

MOTHER. Then get on with it! And while you're at it, you can tell me why you vanished off the face of the earth without saying a word! And why you took all our money with you! Every last penny we had in the world!

FATHER. I didn't tell you what I was doing because I was scared if I talked about it I would lose my nerve . . . It wasn't a spur of the moment thing . . . I've been thinking about it a long time, dreaming about it . . . All those years working in a factory . . . It's funny really, if I hadn't lost my job, I'd never have dared do it, not in a million years . . .

MOTHER. I'll go off my head!

MICHAEL. Dad, whatever you've done, you have to tell us . . . You have to tell us now.

FATHER. Yes . . . I suppose I do . . . I've missed you, you know . . .

MICHAEL. Dad!

FATHER. Yes, all right . . . (*After a deep breath.*) There's someone I want you to meet. She's called Peggy Sue. She's been looking forward to meeting you . . . I've told her all about you . . .

He pulls away the sheets to reveal a gleaming yacht with the name Peggy Sue *painted on her hull.* MICHAEL *and his* MOTHER *stare in amazement.*

So there you are . . . What do you think?

MOTHER (*utterly stunned*). She's a yacht.

MICHAEL. She's fantastic!

FATHER. I've had her checked out. She's a Bowman. Best make, best design there is, and the safest . . .

MOTHER (*still unable to take it in*). She's a yacht.

FATHER. You know what I couldn't take? After the factory closed the only wage coming into our house was Michael's paper round.

MICHAEL. I didn't mind . . .

FATHER. I know you didn't, but I did, it drove me mad, and so I started to think – what's always been the most special thing for us? Sailing our dinghy on Sundays, right? All three of us and Stella on the reservoir. And then I thought, why not make our whole life special, not just Sundays? We've got the redundancy money, there's a bit saved, the money I got from the car . . . I know, we could do what everyone else does and put it in the bank, but what for? Just to watch it dribble away until there's nothing left? Or we could do something really special with it, a once-in-a-lifetime thing – we could sail around the world. Africa, South America, Australia, the Pacific. We could see places we've only dreamed of.

MOTHER. Around the world?

FATHER. I know – you're thinking we've only ever sailed a dinghy, he's gone crazy, it's too dangerous, we'll be flat broke . . .

MOTHER. I'm not leaving my home. I was born there. I'm not leaving.

FATHER. It wouldn't be for ever . . . A year, maybe eighteen months . . . And we'll train before we go . . . Learn to be proper sailors. You, Mum, you'll do your yachtmaster's certificate. Oh, didn't I say? You'll be skipper, Mum. I'll be first mate and handyman. Michael, you'll be cabin boy, and Stella, I know it's a terrible insult, but you'll have to be ship's cat. A few months training, and we'll be off round the world, Linda, the world! What do you think?

MICHAEL. Fan-tas-tic!

But his MOTHER *has not given her reply.*

FATHER. It'll be the adventure of a lifetime. It's our one chance, Linda. We'll never get another. What do you say?

MOTHER (*after a pause*). I'll be skipper, you say?

FATHER/MICHAEL (*in unison*). Aye, aye, cap'n.

MOTHER. What about Michael's school?

FATHER. We'll take books. Plotting our course will be his Maths, he can keep a logbook for his English. I'll teach him. You'll teach him. He'll learn more at sea than he ever would in that monkey school of his.

MICHAEL. That's true, Mum, I promise that's true.

MOTHER. I don't know . . . (*But she's smiling now.*) Go ahead. Buy her. Buy the boat.

FATHER. I already have.

MOTHER. What did you say?

FATHER. I already have.

MOTHER (*going for him*). One of these days, I'll kill you, James Farrow . . . I swear I will, I'll wring your neck . . .

But she embraces him instead, and he hugs her back.

FATHER. A hug is one thing . . . Look away, Michael, I'm afraid I'm going to have to kiss your mother.

MICHAEL. Do you have to?

FATHER. 'Fraid so . . .

MICHAEL *smiles and covers his eyes, and* FATHER *kisses* MOTHER *tenderly.*

MOTHER. Here's to us, then – The Lunatic Family!

ALL (*in unison*). The Lunatic Family!

MOTHER. Oh, no! I've just thought of something – what's Granny going to say?

Scene Two

GRANDMOTHER (*loud, withering*). Sailing a yacht? Around the world? You're cracked, all of you! Flipped your lid! I've never heard anything so ridiculous!

MICHAEL, *his* MOTHER *and* FATHER, *with* STELLA *on board, learn to sail the* Peggy Sue. *They attempt some sailing drills, but fail badly, narrowly avoiding injury. As they struggle to master timing and teamwork, and gain control over ropes, winches and sails, their* GRANDMOTHER *continues to pour heavy scorn down on them.*

And who do you think you are? Yachts are like racehorses . . . They're what rich people do! Millionaires, dukes and princes! They're not for ordinary folk! Ordinary folk don't do things like that! Ordinary folk do not sail yachts! You'll lose everything, and what will you do then, tell me that? Saltwater doesn't buy shoes, you mark my words, life isn't a fairy tale! It's not a Hollywood film! You need to learn your proper place in life!

There is a marked improvement in their drills.

And I don't care how many weeks and months you spend pulling ropes and shouting orders, you'll never learn how to sail it properly! You'll sink before you leave port! You'll be a laughing stock! You'll be on the news! You'll win the prize for being The Biggest Fools Of The Year! You listen to your grandmother! I've lived longer than you so I know

more than you do! Stop this nonsense, now! Stop it before
someone gets hurt!

MICHAEL *and his* MOTHER *and* FATHER *work with real
precision and teamwork. What at first seemed impossible,
now seems almost routine.* MOTHER *goes.* FATHER *and*
MICHAEL *work on the boat, preparing her for sea.*

And even if you do make it out to sea . . . If your own
stupidity doesn't sink you first, there are lots of other things
that will! Icebergs, pirates, seasickness, hurricanes, whales,
supertankers, sharks, squids, tsunamis, monsters of the deep!

MOTHER *returns, holding something behind her back.*

FATHER (*nervous, the stakes are high*). Well, how did you get
on?

MOTHER. Okay, I suppose . . .

MICHAEL. What do you mean, 'okay'?

FATHER. Did you pass or didn't you?

MOTHER *takes out a certificate from behind your back.*

MICHAEL. Your yachtmaster's certificate! You've done it,
Linda! You've really done it. Now, there's nothing to stop
us . . . Nothing at all . . . (*A little in awe of their hard-won
freedom.*) We can go wherever we like . . .

GRANDMOTHER (*indefatiguable*). You're done for, I tell
you! I brought you into the world, and now I have to watch
you throw your lives away on a crack-brained scheme
dreamed up by a man with a cracked brain . . . He never
was good enough for you, Linda . . . If you'd listened to
me . . .

MOTHER. Granny?

GRANDMOTHER. What?

MOTHER/FATHER/MICHAEL (*in unison*). Shut up!

MOTHER. Right then, first mate, cabin boy, ship's cat, say
goodbye to all you know – a week today, we sail on the
morning tide!

Scene Three

Friends and families, unseen on the shore, shout out their best wishes as the Peggy Sue *prepares to set sail.*

MICHAEL (*calling to shore*). Goodbye, Grannie . . . Goodbye, Eddie . . . Come on then, throw it . . . (MICHAEL *catches a football.*) Mum, Dad, look what Eddie's given me . . . (*Shouting to shore.*) You're a headcase, Eddie – what use is a football on a boat? (*To his parents.*) Look, he's even signed it . . . (*Reading.*) To Mikey, with lots of luck. Your best friend. Eddie Dodds. (*Shouting to shore.*) You are my best friend, Eddie . . . (*Holding up football.*) One day I'll play football with this in Brazil . . . In Brazil! Goodbye, Eddie . . . Goodbye, everyone . . . Goodbye . . .

They set sail, with MOTHER *at the helm. The shouts of farewell recede into silence, and* MICHAEL *and his* MOTHER *and* FATHER *fall silent too, overwhelmed by their own daring.*

FATHER (*a sudden panic*). A motorboat!

MOTHER. I see it!

FATHER. Another one! Watch your line!

MOTHER. I'm fine . . . Stop panicking . . . We'll never get anywhere if you keep panicking . . .

FATHER. I'm not panicking . . . I'm amazed . . . I'm completely amazed . . . Look!

MICHAEL (*quietly, moved*). The open sea . . . We've done it . . . This isn't a dream, is it? This is real . . . Really real . . .

FATHER. God forgive me if anything happens to either one of you . . .

MOTHER. I'm your skipper, and I'm not going to let anything happen . . . I'm your skipper, and I'm going to take you round the world . . . Do what I tell you, and you'll see everything you've ever dreamed of . . . Do you hear me?

MICHAEL/FATHER (*in unison*). Aye, aye, cap'n.

MOTHER. Right, then – James, take the wheel and I'll check
  our course, Michael, make the lunch, and after we've eaten
  you can begin your logbook . . .

MICHAEL. Aw, Mum . . .

MOTHER. We'll start as we mean to go on! Every day you'll
  write a page, and every night you'll read it to us. You've got
  school books for your coursework, and I want you to note
  down and draw all the birds and fish we see. And every
  morning you'll fill in longitude and latitude in the ship's
  log.

MICHAEL. Every morning?

MOTHER. We need to know where we are. That's how we
  stay alive. Is that understood?

MICHAEL (*muttering*). It's gone to her head . . .

MOTHER. What was that?

MICHAEL. Nothing.

MOTHER. Just as well, now get on with it!

MICHAEL (*grudgingly*). Aye, aye, skipper.

  MOTHER *and* FATHER *work quietly on deck. A radio*
  plays very quietly. MICHAEL *takes out his logbook, sits*
  down by STELLA.

It's all right for some . . . All you do is eat and sleep and
stick your nose into the wind . . . (*She licks his face.*) Yuk,
hot dog-breath . . . (*Reads from his logbook.*) 'September
the twentieth. We left Southampton five days ago. The
Channel was full of tankers, so Mum or Dad took all the
turns on watch for the first two nights. It's five in the
morning. I'm on my first watch in the cockpit, and no one
else is awake. I love it, with the *Peggy Sue* on her windvane
self-steering, Mum and Dad asleep below, Stella lying at
my feet. Gazing up at the stars, I feel sometimes that we're
the last people alive on the whole planet. There's just us and
the dark sea and the millions of stars above . . . '

FATHER. Hey, Monkey-Face, I thought you were supposed to be rubbish at English . . .

MICHAEL. I am rubbish at English . . . (*Reading.*) 'Last night I had my nightmare again of falling overboard and watching the *Peggy Sue* sailing away without . . . '

MOTHER. I don't want to hear that, Michael.

She shivers.

MICHAEL. But it's true . . .

MOTHER. It's not true, it's only a bad dream. Read something else.

MICHAEL. 'October the third. We saw dolphins again today, diving in and out of the waves right beside us, as if they were giving us an escort. I always thought if I died I'd like to come back as a bird, but now I think I'd rather be a dolphin . . . '

FATHER. You are not rubbish . . . That was really good . . . Better than the radio.

MOTHER. We look forward to hearing you read.

MICHAEL. This is different. At school I could never think of what to write or how to begin. But out here, on the *Peggy Sue*, I open up my book and it just happens . . . There's so much to do and see, it's not like I write it down at all . . . It's more like I say it . . . Speak it from my head, down my arm, through my fingers and my pencil, and out onto the page . . .

FATHER. Well, you're doing great, son, really great.

MOTHER. Read some more . . .

MICHAEL (*reading*). 'October the fourth. Two full weeks at sea and all's well, except for having to eat baked beans all the time . . . Dad's farts are so loud they'll be heard all the way . . . '

FATHER. I take it all back . . .

MOTHER. Well, it's true.

FATHER. You're one to talk.

MOTHER. Don't be ridiculous.

FATHER. We don't need the wind to blow us along . . . You do that all by yourself . . .

MOTHER (*suddenly urgent*). Ssh, be quiet! (*Turns up the radio.*) Listen!

The tail end of a storm warning plays on the radio.

That was our position, I'm sure of it . . . Batten down . . . Haul in the sails . . . Hurry now!

FATHER. It feels all right to me . . .

A wind gets up.

MOTHER. Listen to the wind . . . Look at the sky . . . Come on, we have to hurry . . .

A loud crack of thunder, the sound of lashing rain. They hurry to carry out their storm drill, but the storm strikes with savage force before they have completed their tasks. The loose sail swings and flaps dangerously, the boat is tossed by huge waves. STELLA barks in fear. MICHAEL cuddles her, but his MOTHER is struck by the sail, and when MICHAEL goes to help her he loses his footing, and is swept over the side, saved only by his FATHER's desperate grip. After long moments, his FATHER, helped by a frantic MOTHER, succeeds in hauling MICHAEL back on board. They huddle together until the storm blows out. Michael's MOTHER is the first to stand.

(*Fiercely, passionately.*) Let this be a lesson . . . We thought we were God's gift to sailing, and look what happened . . . In the blink of an eye . . . We nearly lost you, Michael . . . Well, it won't happen again, not as long as I'm captain of this boat! We'll wear harnesses at all times . . . Whenever you're on deck, you'll be clipped on. Do you hear me?

Exhausted, and still in shock, they can only mutter their assent.

Well, let me hear it – Aye, aye, cap'n!

FATHER/MICHAEL (*in unison, but wearily*). Aye, aye, cap'n.

MOTHER. Don't act so sorry for yourselves! We're alive, aren't we? Listen to me, the pair of you! By the moon and the stars, I give you my word – Storms will come and storms will go, but we'll always still be here, still alive and still afloat. (*She embraces them both.*) Now, take a shake to yourselves, for heaven's sake! There's work to do!

Scene Four

A fine, clear night. The Peggy Sue, *under self-steering, sails on smoothly. Swaying lamps cast a magical light.* MICHAEL *and his* MOTHER *and* FATHER *all wear clipped-on safety harnesses.* MICHAEL *sits with his logbook, with* STELLA *by his side. His* MOTHER *and* FATHER *play chess.*

MICHAEL (*reading from his logbook*). 'October the eighth. Mum gets quite snappy sometimes when we don't do things right. Dad just winks at me and we get on with it. They play a lot of chess when it's calm enough. Dad's winning so far.'

FATHER. Checkmate! (*Punches the air.*) Yes, yes, yes! The Grand-master takes a convincing lead – nine games to five.

MICHAEL. 'Mum says she's not bothered.'

MOTHER. It's only a game, for heaven's sake.

MICHAEL. 'But she is, I can tell . . . We only spent two days in La Coruna. Mum slept a lot. She had cramps in her stomach. Dad did some work on the rudder cable, and now we're on the way to the Azores. I can't stand the sight of baked beans, and there's still boxes of them down below.'

FATHER. This is the life . . . Whose idea was this anyway?

MOTHER. Hurry up, it's your move.

FATHER. Well, whoever thought it up must be a great man. (*Plays his move.*) Don't you think, Linda? A wonderful husband, a genius, a man of vision . . .

MOTHER. Checkmate!

She applauds herself, punches the air.

MICHAEL. 'October the eleventh. Today I saw Africa! It was in the distance but Mum said it was definitely Africa.'

MOTHER. We're going down the West coast. The wind will take us a few hundred miles down the coast and then across the Atlantic to South America. We mustn't drift off course, or we'll end up in the Doldrums. There's no wind there at all, and we could just sit there becalmed for weeks, or maybe for ever.

FATHER tunes the radio, finds a station playing a slow samba.

FATHER. May I have this dance?

MOTHER. It'll be my pleasure, Señor.

They dance together slowly and lovingly.

MICHAEL. 'November the sixteenth. I've played football in Brazil! Do you hear that, Eddie? And I played on the beach with your lucky football. Out team lost five–three, mainly because Dad was in goal. If you'd been there we'd have won easy.'

The radio plays a Christmas carol – a familiar tune, but the words are sung in Portuguese.

'December the twenty-fifth. Christmas Day at sea. We had the Christmas pudding Gran made for us, but it was horrible.'

FATHER. That was heavier than a cannonball! I think I'm going to die.

MOTHER. Even Stella wouldn't touch it, and she eats dead seagulls.

MICHAEL. 'We passed south of an island called St. Helena. No need to stop. Nothing there, except it's the place where Napoleon was exiled. He died there. A lonely place to die.'

MOTHER. Checkmate! Twenty-one games to twenty! She's in the lead! For the first time, she's in the lead!

FATHER. I thought you said it was only a game.

MOTHER. For some it is. For others it's a mixture of philosophy and art.

She punches the air.

MICHAEL. 'January the first. New Year's Day, and it's Africa again! Cape Town. Table Mountain.'

FATHER. This time we'll put into port. We'll go on safari.

MOTHER. Do you hear that, Michael? We're going to see elephants and lions in the wild. I never though life could be so good. Oh, I love this!

MICHAEL. 'They were like a couple of kids, all laughing and happy. They were never like this at home. These days they really smile at each other.'

MOTHER. My husband, my son, my best friends.

FATHER. Don't overdo it. We are British subjects, after all.

MOTHER. Not any more we're not – we're citizens, citizens of the world!

She embraces and kisses him.

MICHAEL. 'February the seventh. Hundreds of miles out in the Indian Ocean. I still dream of the elephants I saw in Africa.'

FATHER. I loved how slow they were, so slow and thoughtful.

MOTHER. I loved their wise, weepy eyes.

FATHER. Next stop Australia. Uncle John's going to meet us in Perth.

MICHAEL. Who's Uncle John?

FATHER. A distant uncle.

MOTHER. Very distant.

FATHER. Oh, ha ha, very funny.

MICHAEL. 'May the third. Australia was such a brilliant place
we stayed for three months. Mum saw a doctor about her
stomach cramps, and she's much better now. He said it was
probably something she ate. Dad reckons it was Granny's
Christmas pudding. I saw a snake called a copperhead.
Uncle John said it could have killed me if I'd trodden on it.
He told us to watch out for redback spiders in the toilet.
Mum said . . .'

MOTHER. Right, that's it! I'm never going to the toilet again!

MICHAEL. You'll have to, you can't not go to the toilet.

MOTHER. I don't care! I'll wear a nappy, I'll pee in a jug . . .

MICHAEL. But you can't . . .

MOTHER. I won't hear another word!

MICHAEL. 'I looked every time, but I never saw a single spider.'

MOTHER (*patting* STELLA). Poor Stella, your collar's worn
through . . . That reminds me, I need to make a special
harness for you . . . (*Kisses* STELLA.) We couldn't lose
you, could we, my love?

She grimaces in pain.

FATHER. What's wrong, Linda? It's cramps again, isn't it?

She nods.

We should go back and see another doctor.

MOTHER. Nonsense, that would be giving in. Just think –
England to Australia, halfway around the world!

FATHER. And we've done it all on our own.

MOTHER. Here's to us, then – The Lunatic Family!

ALL (*in unison*). The Lunatic Family!

FATHER *at the wheel.* MOTHER, *looking ill and exhaused,
sits with* STELLA.

MICHAEL. 'June the thirteenth. It's a dark, dark night. No
moon. No stars. But it's calm again at last. We've had a
terrible time ever since we left Sydney.'

FATHER (*to* MICHAEL, *quietly, so that* MOTHER *won't hear*). This is the worst it's ever been, Michael. It's just been storm after storm, and each one blows us further north across the Coral sea. The rudder cable has snapped. I've done what I can, but the self-steering doesn't work any more, so someone's got to be at the wheel all the time. And that means you or me because Mum's much worse this time. Do you understand, Michael? It's you and me.

MICHAEL. I understand, Dad.

FATHER. Good boy.

MICHAEL (*speaking what he's now writing in his logbook*). 'Mum hasn't been able to look at the charts for three days. Dad and I have been doing the navigation. We've been doing our best but, if we're honest, I don't think we know where we are any more.'

FATHER. Michael?

MICHAEL. I've got it, Dad.

MICHAEL *takes the wheel.*

FATHER. I'll take over in two hours. (*To* MOTHER.) Come on, I'll take you below. You need to sleep.

MOTHER. I'll be all right.

FATHER. I know you will, but you need to sleep . . .

He helps her go below.

MOTHER. Goodnight, Michael.

MICHAEL. Goodnight, Mum.

MOTHER. My husband, my son, my best friends . . .

She goes below.

FATHER. You are a good boy, you know that . . . (*Ruffles* MICHAEL*'s hair.*) The best . . . Goodnight, son . . .

MICHAEL. Goodnight, Dad.

His FATHER *goes below.*

We need Mum to get better, Stella, or we're in real trouble. I don't think we could stand another storm. Thank God it's calm. It'll help Mum sleep . . .

STELLA *has gone up to the bow, where she begins to bark.*

Be quiet, Stella, you'll wake Mum. Come here, girl, come on.

But she ignores him and keeps barking.

Come on then, come and get the ball . . .

He leaves the wheel, kneels down and rolls the ball from hand to hand.

Come on, come and play, come and get the ball . . .

He loses control of the ball, and it rolls over the side.

Look what you've done! You've made me lose it! I've lost my lucky ball!

The sound of mysterious singing from the surrounding darkness.

What's that sound? Is that what you're barking at, Stella?

STELLA *barks.* MICHAEL *calls out.*

Who's there? Is there anyone there? No one . . . Listen, Stella, it's stopped, whatever it was . . .

But STELLA *keeps barking.*

I've told you, you'll wake Mum . . . Come here, come on . . .

But she won't come.

You stupid dog . . .

He unclips his harness.

Now, come here, you daft thing . . . Come here . . .

He takes her by the collar, but the collar breaks, and she won't be moved.

Then I'll just have to carry you . . .

He bends, puts his arm around STELLA, *and the boat veers. With his arms full, he can't grab the guard rail, and*

MICHAEL *and* STELLA *plunge overboard. Under water,*
MICHAEL *holds his breath, and only calls out when he*
surfaces, gasping for air.

Mum! Dad! Help, Mum!

He submerges again, holding his breath. The Peggy Sue
sails slowly away. He bursts to the surface.

Oh, God, Mum! Dad! I'm here! I'm here! Mum . . . Dad . . .

He chokes, struggles for air, loses contact with STELLA.
The Peggy Sue *vanishes.*

Mum! Dad . . . I'm so sorry . . . Oh God, please . . . Mum . . .
Dad . . . Dad . . .

Fade to darkness. The sound of mysterious singing.

Scene Five

The sound of waves and seabirds. MICHAEL *lies unconscious*
on a wide, white sweep of beach. A howling from the trees
becomes a screaming, a fearful crescendo of screeching.
MICHAEL *stirs and wakes. The screeching dies away in its*
own echoes. MICHAEL *coughs painfully.*

MICHAEL. Sand . . . Water . . . It can't be . . . I'm on a boat . . .
(*Closes his eyes.*) I'm asleep and dreaming on a boat . . .
Mum, Dad? (*Opens his eyes.*) Oh no . . . No . . . No . . .
There's nothing . . . No one . . .

STELLA *enters and bounds over to him, leaping and*
licking. MICHAEL *hugs her.*

Stella! It's so good to see you . . . So good . . . I thought I
was alone . . . Don't worry, girl . . . We're alive, aren't we?
That's what Mum would say . . . We're alive . . .

He stands shakily, and looks around.

Nothing . . . Just sand and trees and water and sky . . .
They'll find us, Stella, I know they will . . . (*Calling out.*)

Mum, Dad . . . Mum, Dad . . . Where are you? Mum, Dad, Mum, Dad, Mum . . .

He calls and calls until tears come and he can call no more. He drops to his knees. STELLA *drops a stick, wanting* MICHAEL *to throw it.*

Look at you, you daft thing . . . My biggest nightmare's come true and you want me to throw a stick . . . It's easy being a dog, but maybe you're right . . . What use are tears? They just make your face wet . . .

A plaintive howling comes from the trees.

Listen, Stella . . . I've heard that noise before . . . At the zoo . . . (STELLA *barks*.) Quiet, girl . . . We'll be all right . . . Mum and Dad'll come back for us . . . They won't leave us here . . . They'll look until they find us, you'll see . . . All we've got to do is keep a lookout for them, and stay alive. Water, we'll need water, but so do those animals, right? We've just got to find it, that's all. And there must be food too, fruit or nuts or something. We'll eat what they eat . . . Come on, Stella . . . We'll climb that hill, and then we'll get a view of where we are . . .

He climbs through the trees with STELLA *close by.*

Look up there . . . Coconuts, but they're too high to reach, and the trunks are too smooth to climb . . . Still at least there's some shade . . . You can see from here, it's an island . . . It must be a mile long and a mile across . . . But I can't see a stream . . . There must be water, there must be . . .

STELLA *gives a low growl.*

Can you feel it too? Something's watching us, following us . . .

Finds his penknife in his pocket.

My penknife! Well, it's something, I suppose . . . Don't be frightened, Stella, that'll just make them worse . . . Over there! Something moved! Come on, Stella, quickly! Back to the beach! Quickly!

They run back to the beach.

It's so hot, the sun'll cook us . . . We've got to find water, we've got to . . .

He becomes aware that STELLA *is drinking.*

No, Stella, don't drink seawater. You go mad if you do that . . . It's in a bowl . . . It's not seawater! And here's another one!

He finds another battered tin bowl set higher on a piece of driftwood. He drinks deeply and thankfully.

I never knew water could taste so good . . . What's this? Palm leaves, but there's something underneath . . . Fish, lots of them laid out in rows! And bananas, little red bananas! The fish is raw! Do you care, Stella? I don't . . . Here you are, some for you, some for me . . .

He eats hungrily, sharing the fish with STELLA.

They're delicious! We'll share the fish, but I'll have the bananas . . .

He calls out in between mouthfuls of fish.

Thank you, whoever you are . . . Thank you, thank you, thank you . . .

His words echo round the island, and the forest replies with a cacophony of singing and hooting and howling and cawing and croaking.

And hullo to you too! There must be people as well, Stella . . . They must have put out the food and water for us . . . They must be watching, looking after us . . . And look, in the sand . . . Something shining . . .

He picks up the shining object, drops it immediately.

Ouch, it's hot!

Picks it up with the cuff of his shirt.

A piece of glass . . . Brilliant! We can make fire! Eddie showed me how to do it . . . All you need are dry leaves and twigs . . .

He hurries to gather up leaves and twigs, gathers them in a heap.

It's bound to work with the sun this hot. Think, Stella, we can sleep by the fire at night, it'll keep away the flies and animals, and in the daytime someone's got to see the smoke . . . We've got food, water and fire . . . We're going to be all right, Stella . . .

Calls out.

Thank you for the fish and bananas . . . My name is Michael. I fell off a boat. Who are you? Show yourself, I'd like to know who you are . . . Show yourself . . .

A huge orang-utan bursts out of the trees and lumbers towards MICHAEL, who drops the piece of glass onto the leaves, and falls back in shock. STELLA crouches and growls.

Quiet, Stella, don't growl . . .

The orang-utan sits down just a few feet from MICHAEL, scratches lazily, considers MICHAEL. MICHAEL does not dare look the creature in the eye.

We're friends, aren't we? (*To* STELLA.) Quiet, Stella! (*Quietly, to the orang-utan.*) We are friends. I won't hurt you, and you . . . You won't hurt me . . . I'll be your friend, if you'll be mine.

He risks raising his head slowly, and looking carefully at the orang-utan. The ape immediately seems to take exception, and rushes at him, sniffing him, eyeballing him, forcing MICHAEL to look down and stay absolutely still. Then, happy that she has asserted her dominance, she scratches himself and lumbers back into the trees.

Gone . . . We're alive, Stella, we're still alive . . .

His fire begins to smoke.

Smoke! It's working! It's really working!

He removes the piece of glass from the pile of leaves and twigs, bends and blows on the fire to help it catch.

More wood! Quickly, we need more wood!

*He rushes to gather up more driftwood. Unseen by him, a
figure appears from the smoke, as silent as a ghost. He's no
bigger than* MICHAEL, *and very old. His hair and beard
are long, wispy and white. He wears tattered breeches,
bunched at his waist, with a knife in his belt. He brandishes
a stick, his whole body shakes with fury, and his wild eyes
are accusing and angry.*

OLD MAN (*screeching in fury*). Dameda! Dameda!

MICHAEL *backs away in fear.*

MICHAEL. I don't understand. I'm Michael, who are . . .

OLD MAN. Dameda! Dameda!

MICHAEL *takes another step away from him, but*
STELLA, *to* MICHAEL'*s surprise, goes to the* OLD MAN
as if he's an old friend.

MICHAEL. Stella? Come away . . .

But STELLA *is happy to stay with the* OLD MAN.

OLD MAN. Americajin? Americajin? American? Eikokujin?
British?

MICHAEL (*relieved to have understood something at last*).
English, I'm English . . .

OLD MAN. No good! Fire no good! You understand? No fire!

MICHAEL. But my mother, my father, they might see it, see
the smoke. (*He points out to sea by way of explanation.*)
Out there. They're out there. They'll see the fire. They'll
come and find me . . .

OLD MAN (*again shrieking in fury*). Dameda! Dameda! (*He
lifts his stick as if he might strike* MICHAEL.) No fire . . .

*He turns away, and kicks apart the pile of smoking leaves,
putting out the fire.*

MICHAEL. You can't do that! That's mine!

OLD MAN. Dameda!

MICHAEL. Shout all you like, that's my fire!

OLD MAN. Dameda! No fire!

He begins to draw in the sand with his stick, jabbering incomprehensibly all the time.

MICHAEL. What are you doing? It's the island, isn't it? A map of the island . . .

OLD MAN. I Kensuke . . . Kensuke's island . . . (*He divides his map into two areas.*) You boy, you here! I, Kensuke, I here! But no fire! This my island! How say in English? King, I king! And king say no fire! (*Points his stick at* MICHAEL *with fierce, unwavering conviction.*) This Kensuke's Kingdom! No fire! No one come Kensuke's Kingdom! No one! Not ever! Dameda! Dameda!

End of Act One.

ACT TWO

Scene One

The beach. Evening. A crudely-fashioned shelter of driftwood and palm leaves. Enter MICHAEL *with* STELLA. *He carries a branch which he has sharpened with his penknife into a spear for spearfishing. His clothes are now dirty and torn, and his hair is wild and tangled. His arms and legs are marked by bites and scratches. The sun has browned him.*

MICHAEL. How many fish did we catch, Stella? Not one! And how many days is it now?

Checks on the driftwood where he has cut the days.

Thirty-seven . . . Thirty-seven days and not one fish, but whenever he goes spearfishing, the great King Kensuke, he catches loads . . . I've watched him . . . He's quick as a flash and he hardly ever misses . . . You're a good dog, Stella, you found fresh water, but we still have to wait for him to feed us . . .

Scratches at his skin, slaps at his worst mosquito bites.

And every night I get eaten alive by mosquitoes . . .

Scratches and slaps in desperation, and real distress.

I don't think I can stand another night . . . I'll go off my head.

The huge orang-utan appears. MICHAEL *is cautious, but pleased to see her and* STELLA, *used to her now, doesn't bark or growl.*

It's you! It's good to see you, you big lump . . . Are you going to sit down? Come on, then, come on . . . That's it . . . We're friends now . . .

She sits down companionably, scratches herself as if in imitation of MICHAEL.

Do they bite you too? You poor thing . . . How can you ever sleep? It's funny . . . I mean, I know you're an animal, but when I look in your eyes, you look back exactly the same way I look at you . . . If only you could talk . . . Maybe you do, and it's just that I can't speak your language . . .

MICHAEL *imitates some of her grunts and howls, and immediately the orang-utan shows puzzlement followed quickly by keen interest, coming in close, sniffing* MICHAEL, *and leaning over him in a dominant way.*

I didn't mean anything, honest, I didn't . . . Get off, will you? I was only being daft, I was only mucking about . . . Get off . . .

Now that MICHAEL *is speaking his own language again, the orang-utan relaxes, and leaves him alone.*

But where's the little lump? He's never far away from you . . . He's trying to take me by surprise again, isn't he?

MICHAEL *looks around carefully, calling out.*

Come on, I'm ready for you . . . Show yourself . . . You won't sneak up on me this time . . . No one . . .

The orang-utan's baby is about the same size as MICHAEL. *He rushes out of the trees and charges at* MICHAEL, *screeching and howling.* MICHAEL *laughs at his frantic energy.*

It's all right, I see you . . . You're a madman, yes you are, but it's all right . . .

The baby scampers around MICHAEL, *jumps on his back, and seems to howl with laughter and triumph. His* MOTHER *watches without the slightest concern.*

Right, you've asked for it!

MICHAEL *kneels, pulls the baby orang-utan off his back and wrestles playfully with him.*

All right, you win. Do you hear me, you win.

At last the baby calms down. He sits looking intently at MICHAEL. *He checks through* MICHAEL's *hair for bugs, examines his ears, his nose, his ragged shirt. He reaches into the breast pocket of* MICHAEL*'s shirt and takes out the piece of glass.*

Hey, now, that's mine . . . Give it back . . .

The baby sniffs the piece of glass, holds it in his teeth, examines it with curiosity.

You've got to give it back . . . Please, you've got to . . . It's not just a piece of glass, it's fire . . . I can light a fire with that . . . Please . . .

MICHAEL *goes to snatch it back, but the baby is too quick for him.* MICHAEL *chases the baby, catches him, and tries to get the piece of glass back by force, but he's neither quick or strong enough.* MICHAEL *becomes frustrated and angry.* STELLA *begins to bark and circle* MICHAEL *and his opponent.*

I'm warning you, you furry bag of fleas! If you don't give me that back I'll . . .

The mother orang-utan, as if sensing that a fight is brewing, charges at them, grunting and chattering. She separates them instantly, and rounds on her son, holding out her hand for the piece of glass. He turns away mischievously as if to say 'You must be joking'. His mother growls fiercely and adopts an intimidating, aggressive posture, and immediately her son gets the message, and surrenders the piece of glass. She turns, sniffs the glass, and offers it to MICHAEL.

Oh, thank you, thank you . . .

But as he goes to take it, she whisks it away.

Oh, no, not you too . . . You don't understand . . . It's my secret . . . This isn't really a shelter . . . Look, it's my secret fire . . . The old man doesn't know, but I'm going to light it as soon as I see a ship . . .

The orang-utan holds out the piece of glass, but whisks it away again as soon as MICHAEL *reaches for it.*

My fire's useless without that piece of glass . . . I need it . . . I really need it . . .

The orang-utan holds it out again, but this time MICHAEL *doesn't reach for it.*

You're worse than Billy Horseborough . . . I'm not falling for it again . . . You can hold it out all you like, but I'm not . . .

As if MICHAEL *has passed some obscure test, the orang-utan surprises* MICHAEL *by reaching forward and dropping the piece of glass back into his shirt pocket. She turns, and together with her son, they amble off back into the trees.* MICHAEL *takes out his piece of glass, kisses it.*

She gave it back . . . As long as we've got this we can do something, and we don't have to do what that old man tells us . . . What's he like, Stella? Never speaks or smiles . . . He must be crazy . . .

Enter KENSUKE, *unseen by* MICHAEL. *He carries more bananas, and fish wrapped in leaves.*

And what gives him the right to tell me what to do? I'm not his slave . . . He's cracked in the head . . . But I'll show him . . .

He sees KENSUKE, *starts with guilty surprise.*

You've come . . . You're so quiet, I never hear you . . .

KENSUKE *places the fish and bananas on the driftwood.*

You've brought food again . . . Thank you . . . We appreciate it, we really do . . .

KENSUKE *turns to go.*

Don't go? Stay and talk, please . . .

KENSUKE *stops, listens, but doesn't look at* MICHAEL.

We'd be dead without you, I know that . . . Who are you? How did you get here? Why are you so angry about a fire? Don't you want to be rescued?

MICHAEL, *in real distress, scratches and slaps at his mosquito bites.*

And how do you ever sleep with all these mosquitoes? They're the worst, they really are . . . I dread the night . . . I do, I dread it more than anything . . .

KENSUKE *looks at* MICHAEL, *then turns to go.*

You can't just go . . . Don't you get lonely?

KENSUKE *goes.*

Come back . . . He's gone, Stella . . . Gone . . . Every time, he just walks away . . . Oh yes, he'll keep me alive but only if I keep to my half of the island and don't light any fires!

Overwhelmed by loneliness and frustration, he shouts out at the top of his voice.

Help me! Somebody help! I'm a prisoner in the middle of nowhere with only a madman for company, a bunch of howling monkeys, a huge orang-utan, and millions of vampire mosquitoes! H-e-e-e-l-p m-e-e-e-e-e!

Once again, it's only the forest that replies with its cacophony of hooting and howling and cawing and croaking. MICHAEL *slumps in despair. Silence falls.* STELLA *comes over to him, licks him gently.*

I know, Stella, I know, you're here . . . You're here . . .

He hugs STELLA.

And there's food, girl . . . Here you are . . . Some for you, and some for me . . .

They eat hungrily.

It's fish again, but we have to eat . . . I remember a teacher saying that eating fish makes you clever . . . Well, we must be geniuses by now . . . (*Yawns.*) Real brainboxes . . . I'm so tired, Stella . . .

He lies back against his shelter/fire.

But I'll never sleep . . . Not with all these mosquitoes . . .

He waves them away sleepily, wraps his arms tightly around himself as if to ward off the mosquitoes.

I'll never . . . sleep . . .

He sleeps. STELLA *settles down beside him.*

FATHER (*calling, from off*). Michael . . . Where are you? Michael . . .

MOTHER (*calling, from off*). Michael . . . Where are you?

MICHAEL (*dreamily*). Mum? Dad?

Enter Michael's MOTHER *and* FATHER.

FATHER. So there you are.

MOTHER. We've found you . . .

FATHER. We've been looking and looking . . .

MICHAEL *stirs*.

MOTHER. We knew we'd find you . . .

FATHER. Come on then, Monkey-face, up onto your feet . . .

MOTHER. It's time you were on your way . . .

MICHAEL (*sitting up*). I'm so sleepy . . .

MOTHER. Hurry, now . . . The boat's waiting . . .

FATHER. There's all your favourite food . . .

MOTHER. Your bed's made up with clean white sheets . . .
Come on, now.

MICHAEL (*getting slowly to his feet*). I'm coming, Mum . . .

FATHER. Hurry up, then . . . Don't be slow . . .

MOTHER *and* FATHER *go*.

MICHAEL. Wait till I tell you . . . There's a funny old
Japanese man who brings me fish, and a huge orang-utan
and her baby . . . He's crazy-mad . . . And I've built a secret
fire . . . Mum? Dad? They've gone . . . Stella . . . Why
haven't you moved? (*It hits him like a blow.*) They were
never here, were they? It was a dream . . . (*Close to tears.*)
They were never here . . .

Enter KENSUKE, *carrying a rolled-up rush mat*.

You? I don't want you! I want my Mum and my Dad! Are
you real, or are you just another stupid dream?

He touches KENSUKE.

You are real . . . Why have you come back? What do you want?

KENSUKE *lays down the rolled-up rush mat.*

KENSUKE. For you . . . Help you sleep . . .

He bows, and vanishes into the night.

MICHAEL. What is it? (*He unrolls the mat, takes out a white sheet sewn into the shape of a sleeping bag.*) It's a sheet! It'll keep out the mosquitoes! (*Shouts out.*) Thank you . . . I don't know if I like you or hate you, but thank you, thank you!

He gets into the sheet sleeping bag, gets comfy.

Oh, that feels so good . . . Come on, Stella, time for a proper sleep.

STELLA *lies down beside him.* MICHAEL *puts his arm around her.*

I wonder if Mum and Dad are dreaming of me . . . If you are, don't worry . . . I've got a sheet, and food, and Stella's here with me . . . (*Sleepily.*) And most important, I'm still alive . . . Goodnight, Mum . . . Goodnight, Dad . . .

He sleeps. Darkness falls.

Scene Two

Morning. The two orang-utans run on, playing a chase game with MICHAEL *and* STELLA. MICHAEL *holds some palm leaves over his head to keep off the fierce sun.*

MICHAEL. It's so hot, we'll be cooked . . . We have to swim! (*Tears off his shirt.*) Come on, race you! Last one in's a hairy ape . . .

He runs into the water, followed by STELLA. *He calls to the orang-utans.*

It feels so good . . . Come on, what are you waiting for?

Enter KENSUKE, *yelling and waving his stick wildly.*

KENSUKE. Yamero! Abunai! No swim! Abunai!

The orang-utans watch him with silent respect, and
STELLA *goes to him welcomingly, but* KENSUKE *is too*
pre-occupied to have any time for animals.

No swim! Dangerous. Understand. No swim!

MICHAEL. Why not? What's wrong?

KENSUKE. Medusa, medusa! Abunai!

MICHAEL. Why do you always have to stop everything? I'll
swim if I want to.

MICHAEL *moves further out into the sea.* KENSUKE
wades angrily out, takes MICHAEL *by the arm and hauls*
him back to shore.

KENSUKE. No swim! Abunai! No swim!

MICHAEL. Let go! That hurts . . . Let go!

KENSUKE. You listen, boy! No swim! Medusa! Danger!

MICHAEL. No, You listen! Let go of me!

KENSUKE *throws him down on the beach.*

KENSUKE. No swim! Very bad! No swim!

KENSUKE *goes, followed by the orang-utans.*

MICHAEL (*stunned and furious, shouting after* KENSUKE).
You're mad, that's what you are! Why can't I swim? What's
so dangerous? Medusa? What's that? I can't see anything!
Look, there's nothing! (*Points and gazes out to sea.*) What's
that? It can't be . . . It is! It's a ship. It's a tanker! (*He jumps*
up and down, waving frantically.) I'm here! I'm here!
They'll never see me . . . The fire! Light the fire!

He rushes to his shelter, pulls away some driftwood to
reveal his carefully concealed pile of dry leaves and small
branches and twigs. He kneels down with his piece of glass,
concentrates on focusing the hot sun.

Come on! Burn, will you, burn! (*He blows on the fire and a thin line of smoke begins to rise.*) That's it, that's it! (*The smoke gets thicker.*) They'll see me now . . . Please let them see me . . . Please God . . . (*He jumps up and down beside his smoking fire.*) I'm here, I'm here!

Enter KENSUKE, *with the orang-utans, unseen by* MICHAEL.

You've got to see me now, you've got to!

He turns back to his fire and sees KENSUKE *staring at him with rage and hurt.* KENSUKE *stamps on the embryo fire, kicking and scattering the leaves and branches.*

Noooo!

KENSUKE *picks up the piece of glass and hurls it into the sea.*

KENSUKE (*with chilling finality*). Dameda! No fire!

MICHAEL. But there's a ship, can't you see? I want to go home. Why won't you let me? Why? I just want to go home.

MICHAEL *is near to tears.* KENSUKE *stares at him, and takes a step towards him as if he might console him, but he stops himself, and instead he bows stiffly from the waist.*

KENSUKE. Gomenasai . . . Gomenasai . . . Sorry . . . So sorry . . .

He goes, followed by the orang-utans.

MICHAEL (*shouting after him*). Sorry? Anyone can say sorry! Sorry, sorry, sorry! Are you watching, old man? I'm going to swim. I don't care what you say. I don't care if you don't feed me. You hear me, old man? (*He runs into the sea.*) I'll do what I want. It's my sea as much as yours.

Enter KENSUKE, *very alarmed.*

KENSUKE. Abunai! Danger! Medusa, medusa!

MICHAEL. It's my sea, and I'll swim if I like! Are you watching, old man? Are you watching?

Suddenly MICHAEL *gasps and twists in pain.*

That hurts! That really hurts!

He staggers, screaming in pain.

Jellyfish! They're huge, and they're everywhere!

He tries to make it back to shore but, lashed by the deadly stings, he falls, screaming in pain. STELLA *barks, unseen creatures howl and gibber, and the cacophony erupts from the forest as if the creatures there are responding to* MICHAEL's *distress.* KENSUKE *picks* MICHAEL *up and carries him away, followed by* STELLA.

Scene Three

KENSUKE's *magical cave-mouth home. With its large white awning, and the chairs and table made from driftwood, his home has an airy, dream-like beauty. There is no clutter. Everything has its place, and its purpose.* KENSUKE *lays* MICHAEL *down on a bed of rushes under the awning. Pale and deeply asleep,* MICHAEL *is wrapped in a white sheet.* STELLA *lies down loyally at* MICHAEL's *feet.*

KENSUKE (*urgently, worried that* MICHAEL *may die*). You no die, boy . . . You no die . . . (*With water in a tin dish, he kneels beside* MICHAEL, *and bathes his head.*) Hear Kensuke . . . You sleep, but you no die . . .

KENSUKE *goes into his cave. The awning flaps gently in the wind. Enter Michael's* MOTHER *and* FATHER. *They call out to him in an everyday way, as if they're calling up to his bedroom at home, from the kitchen downstairs.*

FATHER. Wake up, Monkey-face . . .

MOTHER. Come on, Michael, you'll be late . . .

FATHER. Sleeping your life away . . . You can't stay in your bed all day.

MOTHER. There's a bacon roll and a cup of tea . . .

FATHER. Come on, Lazybones . . .

He goes.

MOTHER (*intimate now, urgently*). We need you to wake up, Michael. Do you hear me?

MICHAEL (*stirring*). Mum, Dad . . .

MOTHER. We need you to wake up . . . (*As she goes.*) By the moon and the stars, I give you my word – Storms will come and storms will go, but we'll always still be here, still alive and still afloat . . . You hear me, Michael . . . You hear me . . .

She's gone.

MICHAEL (*weakly*). I hear you . . .

Enter KENSUKE, *excited.*

KENSUKE. You talk! Boy talk!

STELLA *licks* MICHAEL*'s face.*

MICHAEL (*still dreamily, weakly*). Stella, I love you . . . But no kisses, please no kisses . . . Where am I?

KENSUKE. Kensuke house . . . You sleep for days, I think you die, but now you talk, you move some, you better now . . . I, Kensuke . . . (*Points at* MICHAEL.) You?

MICHAEL. Michael . . . I'm Michael . . .

KENSUKE. Mica.

MICHAEL. Michael.

KENSUKE. Mica.

MICHAEL. Okay, Mica.

MICHAEL *tries to sit up, but groans with pain.*

KENSUKE. No move . . . Still no well . . . Rest and drink . . . (*He lifts up* MICHAEL*'s head, and pours some water down his throat.*) You stay bed till you strong . . . I have gift . . . You wait see . . . (*He produces a painting of a cherry tree on a sheet.*) For you . . . I paint Japan Tree . . . (*He hangs it up.*) I Japanese person . . . Japan tree magic tree . . . Make you better . . .

MICHAEL. Thank you . . . How did you get here? Where did
you get pots and pans, and cups and sheets? Why do you . . .

KENSUKE. No talk . . . Rest, Mica . . . You still poison by
medusa . . .

MICHAEL. Medusa? You mean jellyfish?

KENSUKE. Yes, medusa, sting-fish . . . I fear they kill you . . .
You sleep now . . . Sleep like medicine . . . Make you
strong . . .

MICHAEL (*sleepily*). Sleep . . .

KENSUKE. Tonight bring friends . . . You see . . .

MICHAEL. Friends? You're mad . . . What friends?

He sleeps.

KENSUKE. Good boy, Mica, good boy . . .

Scene Four

Night falls. KENSUKE *lights lanterns, hangs them from the
awning. He places some fruit by* MICHAEL'*s rush bed, gives
a soft call to the darkness, pats* STELLA *to calm her, and then
gently shakes* MICHAEL.

MICHAEL (*staring awake*). Who's there? It's you . . .

KENSUKE. Yes . . . Kensuke here . . .

He goes to give MICHAEL *water.*

MICHAEL. It's all right, I can do it. (*He sits up, takes the cup
and drinks thirstily.*) I can move my hands, and my arms,
and my neck! It doesn't hurt anymore.

KENSUKE (*smiling broadly*). Japan tree magic tree.

MICHAEL (*smiling, nodding*). Japan tree magic tree.
(KENSUKE *hands* MICHAEL *some fruit, and gives
another soft call to the darkness.*) What are you doing?

KENSUKE *puts his finger to his lips, creating a sense of mystery. Slowly the huge orang-utan, answering* KENSUKE'*s call, lumbers into* KENSUKE'*s home.*

KENSUKE. She Tomodachi, she come wish you well.

MICHAEL. Tomodachi . . . That's a better name than big lump . . . It's good to see you, Tomodachi . . .

TOMODACHI *takes some fruit.*

KENSUKE (*scolding her gently*). Aw, Tomodachi, Mica's, Mica's!

MICHAEL. Let her, it's all right . . . When I went to see Uncle Billy in hospital, I ate all his fruit . . . But where's the little lump?

KENSUKE. Ah, Kikanbo, he mad monkey, and he close . . . (*He paces, walking like an ape, searches.*) Kensuke know he close, but where he hide? (

KIKANBO *enters behind* KENSUKE *and walks behind him.* KENSUKE *pretends he doesn't know he's there.*

Where can he be? Is he here?

Looks, but KIKANBO *goes other way.*

Or is he here?

Looks but still does not see him.

He very clever monkey, but I think he . . . (*Spins round suddenly, finds* KIKANBO.) here!

KIKANBO s*creeches, tears around in delight, runs to his mother, and takes her piece of fruit. She cuffs him, and takes the fruit back.*

MICHAEL (*laughing*). Poor Kikanbo. Here, have this.

He offers KIKANBO *another piece of fruit. He takes it and sits by* MICHAEL *as if he's his best friend, and brandishes his piece of fruit at his mother as if his fruit is vastly superior to hers.* TOMODACHI *ignores him, sits at*

KENSUKE*'s feet who seems to be grooming her, plucking out hairs from time to time.*

What are you doing?

KENSUKE (*grinning conspiratorially*). Make brush for painting . . . Tomodachi hair make very good brushes . . .

MICHAEL. That's brilliant! I wish I could paint like you . . . And catch fish like you . . .

KENSUKE. I teach you.

MICHAEL. Will you?

KENSUKE. You must use eyes and ears . . . You must . . .

He can't find any words.

MICHAEL. Look and listen . . .

KENSUKE *nods.*

I will, I promise! (*Pause.*) Kensuke . . . You know how I got here, I fell off a boat, but how did you get here?

KENSUKE (*reluctantly, evasively*). No have words . . . English no good . . .

MICHAEL. Your English is great. How did you learn it?

KENSUKE. When I young man I study Medicine in Tokyo . . . Soon I am doctor, Doctor Kensuke Ogawa . . . Then I go to London, I do studies in London, Guy's hospital . . . Two years I stay, so I learn English words . . . Then I go home to Nagasaki . . . There I have beautiful wife, Kimi, and little son too, Michiya . . . I very happy person in those days . . . But soon war come . . . (*Unable to go on.*) But Mica tired, he must sleep . . .

MICHAEL. I'm not tired . . . Please finish your story . . .

KIKANBO *crawls over beside* MICHAEL, *as if waiting for a bedtime story.*

KENSUKE. Kikanbo, Mica's bed!

MICHAEL. He's okay . . . I think he wants to hear too . . . Please, Kensuke.

Still grooming TOMODACHI *by the light of a hanging lantern,* KENSUKE *tells his story.*

KENSUKE. I am old, but is not long story . . . When war come, I go to Navy . . . I doctor on big warship . . . War go on long time, many Americans come, many planes, many bombs . . . Now war is not so good for Japan . . . We fight but now we lose . . . My ship is bombed . . . Fire and smoke, many men dead, many jump into sea. But I stay. I doctor. I stay with patients . . . Many more bombs come . . . All sailors dead . . . I only one alive on ship but engine still going . . . Ship moving on her own . . . I cannot turn wheel . . . I listen to radio . . . Americans say on radio, big bomb fall on Nagasaki . . . My home . . . Atomic bomb . . . I think my wife Kimi dead, my son Michiya . . . My mother live there too, all my family . . . All dead . . .

MICHAEL. I'm sorry, Kensuke . . .

KENSUKE. Radio say Japan surrender . . . Soon engine stop, but ship not sink . . . Big storm come . . . Sea take ship and bring me here to this island . . . I find food, I find water, but inside I feel bad person, all my family dead, and I alive . . . I want to die . . . But soon I meet apes . . . They very kind to me . . . This very beautiful, very peaceful place . . . No war here, no bad people . . . I take many things from ship . . . Clothes, sheets, pots, bottles, knife, medicine . . . I take everything I find . . . I hide all things in cave . . . Soon ship go down . . . Under water now, under sand . . . My ship part of island now . . .

MICHAEL. But the war was forty years ago!

KENSUKE (*shrugs*). Years come, years go.

MICHAEL. Forty days is bad enough, but forty years? Has no one ever come to find you?

KENSUKE. Some time they come . . . Very bad men . . . Killer men come . . . They have guns . . . They hunt, they shoot . . . I sing to my orang-utans, they come when I sing, most come, all in my cave . . . We hide . . . Killer men not find us, but in forest they shoot mothers, take babies . . . Why must they do this? I think all people killer people . . . I hate all people . . . I not want see people again . . .

MICHAEL. And then I came . . .

KENSUKE. Then Mica come . . . I fishing in boat . . . Wind blow wrong way, sea pull me away very strong . . . When night come I still far away . . . I very frightened . . . I sing . . . It make me brave.

MICHAEL. It was you singing!

KENSUKE. I hear shout, I see light, I think I dream . . . I come quick, I find you and Stella . . .

MICHAEL. And it was you who pulled us out the sea . . . It was you who saved us . . .

KENSUKE. In morning sea bring us again to my island . . . I glad you not dead but I angry too . . . I not want see people . . . I not want you on island . . . I carry you, leave you on beach . . . I give you food and water, but you make fire . . . I not want people find me . . . I not want killer people come . . . Maybe they shoot the apes . . . Maybe they find me, take me away . . . I put out fire . . . I not want see you . . .

MICHAEL. I like the apes too . . . I'm not a killer man . . .

KENSUKE. This true, Micasan, but maybe you bring killer men . . . Then come time when sea full of medusa . . .

MICHAEL. Jellyfish.

KENSUKE. I say not swim, but you very angry so you swim in sea . . . Jellyfish sting . . . I bring you here . . . I have vinegar I make from berries . . . Vinegar kill poison . . . Long time you very sick boy, but you strong again, and we friends now . . . (*Firmly, sternly.*) But no fire, no signal, you promise?

MICHAEL (*with difficulty*). I promise.

KENSUKE. You like son to me now . . . We happy people. We paint. We fish. We stay together. You my family now, Micasan. Yes?

MICHAEL (*moved, meaning it*). Yes, we're family now.

KENSUKE. Good. Now, time to sleep.

KIKANBO *is already asleep.*

MICHAEL. Look, he's sleeping already!

KENSUKE (*whistles, claps his hands*). Kikanbo, Tomodachi, time you go home. Thank you for hair, Tomodachi, make very fine painting brush.

MICHAEL. And thank you for coming to see me. I feel better, I really do . . . Goodnight, Tomodachi . . . Goodnight, Kikanbo . . .

KIKANBO *climbs sleepily into his mother's arms, and she carries him off.* KENSUKE *lays out a rush mat on the ground.*

KENSUKE. Kensuke sleep now . . . Hard for me to talk . . . Make me tired. Very tired . . . Goodnight, Micasan.

He lays down on his mat, falls instantly asleep.

MICHAEL. Goodnight, Kensuke . . . Thank you for telling me your story . . . Kensuke? Asleep . . . (*Goes to table, touches brushes, paints, lifts up an empty bottle. Seized with a sudden energy he dips a brush into some paint and writes quickly on a piece of cloth.*) We are family, and you're very kind, but I have another family . . . A real family . . . Forgive me, Kensuke . . . Forgive me . . .

He rolls up the piece of cloth, puts it in the bottle, screws the top tight shut, and goes silently with STELLA.

Scene Five

Morning. The beach by KENSUKE's *house.* MICHAEL *enters, very excited, carrying his spear and a fish.*

MICHAEL. I've done it, Kensuke, I've done it! I've caught a fish!

Enter KENSUKE.

KENSUKE. Good fish . . . Very good fish . . . Many days you listen to Kensuke and now you very good fisherman person . . . You bring me fish, I bring you this. (*From behind his back, he produces* MICHAEL'*s battered old football.*) For you, Mica.

MICHAEL. My football!

KENSUKE. Found on beach.

MICHAEL. Eddie gave it to me . . . Look, you can still see his name . . . He was my best friend . . .

KENSUKE. Now, I best friend.

MICHAEL (*guiltily*). Yes . . . you are . . .

KENSUKE (*noticing* MICHAEL'*s unease*). Come, Mica, play football . . . (*He dribbles with a frantic energy that belies his years.*) Japan play England . . . Kensuke for Japan, Kensuke kick, Kensuke score! (*He celebrates wildly, but notices that* MICHAEL *is not laughing.*) What wrong, Mica? Days now you no laugh.

MICHAEL. I don't know . . . It's nothing . . .

KENSUKE. Not nothing . . . Say, tell . . .

MICHAEL (*sharply*). I have told you! It's nothing!

Enter TOMODACHI. *She seems sad and worried.*

KENSUKE. Aw, Tomodachi, you still no find Kikanbo . . . (*He whistles, and sings his song to try and bring* KIKANBO.) He very wicked baby . . . He run away a lot . . . Make Tomodachi very sad mother . . .

MICHAEL (*calling*). Kikanbo, Kikanbo! (*Stroking* TOMODACHI.) Poor Tomodachi . . .

KENSUKE. Don't worry, Mica . . . She happy again when he come back . . .

MICHAEL. Kikanbo! He's coming, Tomodachi, it's all right! (*Enter* STELLA, *carrying the bottle in her mouth.*) It's only you, Stella!

STELLA *drops the bottle and looks up, panting and pleased with herself. KENSUKE laughs, and reaches down and picks it up. He understands what it is, and he looks at MICHAEL, not with anger, but with deep hurt. He drops the bottle down at MICHAEL's feet.*

I'm sorry . . . I really am . . . I know I made a promise, but it's nothing, listen . . . (*Opens bottle, takes out message, reads it.*) 'Dear Mum and Dad. I'm alive. I live on an island. I don't know where. Come and find me. Love, Michael.' It was just a stupid idea . . . No one would ever find it . . .

But KENSUKE turns and goes.

Come back! I didn't mean to hurt you . . . I've felt bad ever since I did it . . . Why does everything have to be so hard? I do want to stay here with you, but I want to go home too, I can't help it . . . I'm sorry, Kensuke . . .

Enter KENSUKE. A silence before he speaks.

KENSUKE. It is Kensuke who must say sorry . . . Look how sad Tomodachi when she lose baby . . . Your mother sad too . . . Maybe she look but not find you . . . Think you dead for ever, but see you always in her head . . . I know, I have son Michiya . . . Like Kimi, he dead for sure, but he always in my head . . . I old . . . But you young, want family . . . You can't live on island with old man who die one day . . . So, I change my mind . . . You know what we do tomorrow?

MICHAEL. What?

KENSUKE. We build new, big fire . . . We ready then for when see ship . . . Okay, Micasan?

MICHAEL (*grateful, deeply moved*). Okay . . . Thank you . . .

KENSUKE. But now we do very important thing . . . (*Smiles broadly.*) Japan beat England at football!

He dribbles past MICHAEL who, all guilt gone, joins in, winning the ball back. But, just as he is about to shoot, KIKANBO appears and grabs the ball.

MICHAEL. Kikanbo!

All chase KIKANBO, *even* TOMODACHI *and* STELLA,
*as if they're playing some crazy combination of football and
rugby. But* KIKANBO *is too quick and clever, and he runs
off with the ball, and they chase after him, calling, howling
and laughing.*

Scene Six

MICHAEL *and* KENSUKE *fish from* KENSUKE*'s raft.*
STELLA *lies contentedly.* KENSUKE *watches* MICHAEL *as
he repairs his fishing line.*

KENSUKE. My son . . . Michiya . . . If he live he grown man
now, and my wife Kimi, she seventy-five, same as me . . .
Very beautiful young woman . . . Very beautiful old woman . . .

MICHAEL. Bombs don't kill everyone. They could still be
alive. You could find out . . . You could go home.

KENSUKE (*astonished at the very idea*). Go home? Kensuke
go home? No . . . They dead . . . Atomic bomb very big
bomb, very terrible . . . Americans say Nagasaki is destroyed,
every house . . . My family dead for sure . . . I stay here,
I safe here. I stay on my island.

MICHAEL. There's no war now.

KENSUKE. You sure, Mica?

MICHAEL. Yes, I'm sure, and Japan is a very rich country
now . . . In our house everything electrical, the TV, the
computer, the music players, everything, they all say 'Made
in Japan' on them. Japan makes all the best machines.

KENSUKE. I 'Made in Japan' person . . . Very old person, but
still good, still strong.

MICHAEL (*laughing*). Yes, you are . . . Kensuke, if a ship
does come, and we light our fire, you could come with me . . .
To the world I've told you about . . . A world where man
has landed on the moon, where there are heart transplants,

computers . . . I know! We could fly in Concorde, a plane that goes faster than the speed of sound . . .

KENSUKE. Now you tell fairy tales . . .

MICHAEL. They're not fairy tales . . . It's all true! We could go together.

KENSUKE. Maybe one day I go home . . . Maybe . . . (*Points urgently.*) Look, Micasan!

MICHAEL. What is it? Is it a boat!

KENSUKE. Better than boat. Better than anything. On beach, look!

MICHAEL. Turtles! Thousands of them! And they're so small . . .

KENSUKE. One night every year turtles are born . . . Go down to sea . . . Many years from now, when turtles are big, they come back, they lay eggs again . . . True story, Micasan.

MICHAEL. It's a great story.

KENSUKE (*calling out*). You go to sea, little turtle! You soon be fine big turtle, one day you come back see me . . . (*To* MICHAEL.) They very small, but they very brave, braver than me . . . They do not know what they find out there, but they go anyway . . . Maybe they teach me good lesson . . . When ship come and we light fire, then I go . . . Like turtles, I go . . . I go with you . . .

MICHAEL. I'd like that . . . More than anything . . .

KENSUKE. I go home to Japan . . . Maybe I find Kimi, Michiya . . . I find truth . . . I go with you, Micasan.

STELLA *growls and barks.*

MICHAEL. What's wrong, girl, what is it? (*Peers out to sea.*) There's a boat, Kensuke! The fire, quickly, light the fire!

KENSUKE. First I look, please, Mica . . .

He looks out to sea.

MICHAEL. Come on, we've got to hurry!

KENSUKE. I know this boat . . . I never forget this boat . . .
Killer men come . . . They kill apes and steal babies . . . We
must go quick, Mica, find all orang-utans, bring to cave . . .
They my family, Mica . . . I sing, make them come . . . (*He
sings out, calling to the apes.*) Help me, Mica . . . Help me.

They rush off.

Scene Seven

Outside KENSUKE*'s cave.* MICHAEL *tears down and hides
the awning, and the table. The sound of* KENSUKE*'s singing,
and loud screeching and howling. An orang-utan enters
carrying several infants, and* MICHAEL *ushers them into the
cave.* MICHAEL *rushes off.* KENSUKE *enters, carrying babies,
followed by another orang-utan pulling along a complaining
baby. They all go into the cave, and* MICHAEL *enters,
carrying an armful of baby orang-utans, followed by* STELLA.

MICHAEL. Sssh, keep quiet, or the hunters will hear you . . .
We'll look after you, I promise . . .

He carries them into the cave. KENSUKE *comes out of the
cave, still singing. An adult and a young orang-utan enter,
both carrying babies, and he ushers them urgently into the
cave.* MICHAEL *comes out of the cave.*

KENSUKE. Still many not here . . . Many, many!

MICHAEL. But here's Tomodachi.

Enter TOMODACHI.

Hurry, Tomodachi, this way! (*But she won't move.*) She's
looking for Kikanbo, he's run away again! (*Calling out as*
KENSUKE *sings.*) Kikanbo, Kikanbo, this is not a game,
you've got to come, you've got to . . .

*The sounds of the forest fall silent, replaced with the sound
of an outboard motor which dies. The sound of* MEN*'s
voices, and laughter.*

Kikanbo, where are you?

KENSUKE. Quiet, Mica!

MICHAEL (*to* TOMODACHI, *quietly but urgently*). Come
into the cave now, Tomodachi, now . . . Or they'll see you
and they'll shoot you . . . (*But she won't move. The sound of
voices comes closer.*) There's no time to find Kikanbo!
You've got to come now! She won't move!

KENSUKE *goes to* TOMODACHI, *touches her arm.*

KENSUKE. Kikanbo my son too, he live in my heart, but
come now, old friend . . . Come now . . .

He sings quietly. After a moment, TOMODACHI *goes with*
KENSUKE *and* MICHAEL *into the cave, followed by*
STELLA. *A number of shots ring out. A* HUNTER *enters.
A vicious modern-day pirate, he wears cheap, brightly
coloured clothes, and carries a rifle. He sees the cave,
reloads his rifle, and goes to investigate. Just as he is about
to enter the cave mouth, another* HUNTER *calls to him,
and loud shots ring out. The* HUNTER *turns away from the
cave, shoots at something in the forest, and runs off. More
shots and the sounds of excited voices and laughter, mixed
with the shrieking of captured baby apes. More shots. After
some time, the sound of the outboard motor starting up. It
recedes into the distance, until it can be heard no more.*
KENSUKE, *stricken, comes slowly out of the cave, followed
by* MICHAEL *and* STELLA.

KENSUKE. Many shots, many dead . . . Many young taken
from island . . . I emperor but they kill my people . . .

MICHAEL. But you saved so many . . . They would be dead
without you . . .

KENSUKE (*inconsolable*). They very scared, stay in cave long
time . . . I dig grave now . . . Bury the dead before they
see . . .

MICHAEL. Poor Kikanbo . . . And poor Tomodachi, to lose
her son . . .

Enter KIKANBO, *slowly, silently, shaking with fear.*

Kikanbo!

KENSUKE. You alive, you alive! (*But* KIKANBO *just stands, shaking with fear.*) He think mother dead . . . Tomodachi alive, Kikanbo . . . She alive . . . You see . . .

He sings quietly, and KIKANBO *begins to chatter plaintively. His chattering brings* TOMODACHI *out of the cave.* KIKANBO *runs to his mother, and they embrace.* KENSUKE *takes a spade from the cave mouth, and goes.*

Scene Eight

MICHAEL *paints* TOMODACHI *and* KIKANBO *on a sheet-canvas, putting the finishing touches to the portrait.* STELLA *lies in the shade.*

MICHAEL. Stay still, now . . . Don't move . . . (KIKANBO *moves.*) All right then, move . . . I'm nearly finished anyway . . .

Enter KENSUKE. *He seems older, leaning on his stick.*

KENSUKE. Mica paint for days and days . . . Must be very great masterpiece . . .

MICHAEL. Ha ha . . . There, finished! You can go now . . .

TOMODACHI *and* KIKANBO *go.*

Wait a minute, you haven't been paid . . .

Calls after them, and they come back. He gives them some fruit, kisses them.

Thank you, you were the best, you were brilliant . . .

They go. KENSUKE *examines* MICHAEL*'s painting.*

What do you think?

KENSUKE *can't find the words.*

Well?

KENSUKE (*moved, proudly*). You quick learner, Micasan . . . Already better than Kensuke . . . One day you be very fine painter, like the great Hokusai . . .

MICHAEL. It's for you . . . To say thank you for teaching me . . .
For everything . . .

KENSUKE. For me? I keep?

MICHAEL. Yes, you keep . . .

KENSUKE (*with a bow, accepting the portrait*). Thank you,
Micasan . . . Best present in all my life . . . (*He folds the
painting carefully.*) Now I think you go look out for boat . . .

MICHAEL. I don't want to look . . . I've looked so many times,
month after month, I know a boat will never come . . .

KENSUKE. You young . . . No patience, but ship will come . . .

MICHAEL. So you say . . .

KENSUKE (*pointing out to sea with his stick*). Ship come
now . . .

MICHAEL. Oh yes, very funny . . .

KENSUKE. You look, Micasan . . .

MICHAEL *peers, shielding his eyes against the glare of
the sun.*

MICHAEL. There's something . . . Something white . . . But
it's nothing . . .

KENSUKE. Look again . . .

MICHAEL (*looking again*). A sail . . . Two sails! Two white
sails! The fire, we've got to light our fire!

KENSUKE. I already light fire . . . Look at smoke on hill . . .
That why ship come . . .

MICHAEL (*staring out to sea*). She's a yacht . . . Can't see her
flag . . . Dark blue hull, like the *Peggy Sue* . . . It can't be . . .
It's my mother's cap, I'm sure it is . . . It's the *Peggy Sue*,
Kensuke . . . They've come back for me . . . We're saved,
we're saved!

But KENSUKE *is looking at him solemnly. He puts his hands
on* MICHAEL's *shoulders and looks deep into his eyes.*

KENSUKE. You listen to me very good now, Micasan. I too old for that new world you tell me about . . . My world here . . . If Kimi alive, if Michiya alive, then I be like living ghost coming home . . . I have family here . . . Orang-utan family . . .

MICHAEL. You're not coming, are you?

KENSUKE. Maybe killer men come again . . . Who look after orang-utan? No, I stay on my island . . . This Kensuke's Kingdom . . . Emperor must stay in his kingdom, look after his people . . . Emperor not run away . . . Not honourable thing to do . . .

MICHAEL *begins to cry.* KENSUKE *puts his forehead against* MICHAEL*'s, lets him cry.*

You go now, but before you go, you promise three things. First, you paint every day of life, so one day you be great artist. Second, when you look up at full moon, you think of me, and I do same for you. That way we never forget each other. Last thing you promise very important for me . . . Very important you say nothing of me. You alone here in this place, understand? I not here. After ten years you say what you like, it not matter any more then, I just bones . . . I want no one come look for me . . . I want live in peace. People come, no peace. You understand? You keep secret for me, Mica? You promise?

MICHAEL (*through tears*). I promise.

KENSUKE *smiles, and gives him his football.*

KENSUKE. Take football . . . You very good at football, but very much better painter . . . You go now . . . And you too, Stella . . . (*Embraces* STELLA.) You very good dog, very good friend . . . (*He puts his arm around* MICHAEL *and walks a little distance with him.*) You go . . . (*He turns and walks away from* MICHAEL.) You go now, please . . .

He bows, and MICHAEL *bows back.*

Sayonara, Micasan . . . It has been honour to know you . . . Great honour of my life . . .

MICHAEL *hasn't the voice to reply.* KENSUKE *goes.*

MICHAEL (*after some moments*). Goodbye, Kensuke . . . Goodbye . . .

The sound of Michael's MOTHER *and* FATHER *calling.* STELLA *begins to bark.*

Sssh, it's all right, girl, it's all right . . .

Enter MOTHER *and* FATHER, *staring at* MICHAEL *as if they can't believe their eyes.*

MOTHER. It is you, Michael . . . It's really you . . . We've looked and looked and looked, and we've found you, we've found you . . .

She rushes at him and crushes him in an everlasting embrace.

MICHAEL *looks over at his* FATHER, *who is patting* STELLA.

FATHER (*smiling, through tears*). Hello, Monkey-Face.

Epilogue

2002. An office. Enter MICHIYA OGAWA, *a man in his 50s. He is smartly dressed, successful, perhaps a doctor. He is followed by* MICHAEL, *now a young man of twenty-seven.*

MICHIYA. Thank you for coming all the way to Japan.

MICHAEL. After I got your letter, I had to come. I owe it to your father.

MICHIYA. Until I read your book I thought my father had died in the war. My mother died only three years ago still believing this.

MICHAEL. How did you survive?

MICHIYA. As you say in your book, we lived in Nagasaki, but we were lucky. Before the bomb fell we went into the countryside to see my grandmother . . . And so we lived.

MICHAEL. Your father . . .

MICHIYA. I have no memories of my father . . . Only some photographs, and now your book . . .

MICHAEL. I've brought you something else . . . (*He takes a package out of his bag.*) It's a gift . . . A painting . . . Your father taught me to paint . . .

MICHAEL *unfolds a sheet.*

MICHIYA (*smiling*). On a sheet . . . Like in your book . . .

MICHAEL. Yes, like in my book . . .

MICHAEL *lets the sheet-painting fall open, and holds it up in front of him. It's a life-size painting of* KENSUKE *on the island.* MICHAEL *has clearly obeyed* KENSUKE's *entreaty for the painting shows great skill, and the portrait of* KENSUKE *is strong and vivid and unsentimental.*

MICHIYA (*deeply moved, with a bow*). My father . . .

Despite his reserve, he can't help but step forward and touch the sheet.

My father . . .

He embraces the sheet-portrait, and by embracing the sheet also embraces MICHAEL, *who embraces him back.*

Fade lights.

End.

Glossary

Amerikajin	an American
abunai	danger
dameda	forbidden
Eikokujin	an Englishman
gomenasai	sorry
saayonara	good bye
yamero	stop

Other adaptations for young people from NHB

ANIMAL FARM
Ian Wooldridge
Adapted from George Orwell

ARABIAN NIGHTS
Dominic Cooke

BAD GIRLS
THE LOTTIE PROJECT
MIDNIGHT
SECRETS
THE SUITCASE KID
Vicky Ireland
Adapted from Jacqueline Wilson

BEAUTY AND THE BEAST
Laurence Boswell

A CHRISTMAS CAROL
Karen Louise Hebden
Adapted from Charles Dickens

CINDERELLA
Stuart Paterson

CORAM BOY
Helen Edmundson
Adapted from Jamila Gavin

HIS DARK MATERIALS
Nicholas Wright
Adapted from Philip Pullman

HANSEL AND GRETEL
Stuart Paterson

THE JUNGLE BOOK
Stuart Paterson
Adapted from Rudyard Kipling

KES
Lawrence Till
Adapted from Barry Hines

SLEEPING BEAUTY
Rufus Norris

SUNSET SONG
Alastair Cording
Adapted from Lewis Grassic Gibbon